MAYA ANGELOU

BY JILL KEPPELER

Gareth Stevens
PUBLISHING

Please visit our website, www.garethstevens.com. For a free color catalog of all our high-quality books, call toll free 1-800-542-2595 or fax 1-877-542-2596.

Cataloging-in-Publication Data

Names: Keppeler, Jill.
Title: Maya Angelou / Jill Keppeler.
Description: New York : Gareth Stevens Publishing, 2019. | Series: Heroes of black history | Includes glossary and index.
Identifiers: ISBN 9781538231340 (pbk.) | ISBN 9781538230220 (library bound) | ISBN 9781538233146 (6 pack)
Subjects: LCSH: Angelou, Maya–Juvenile literature. | African American authors–Biography–Juvenile literature. | African American women civil rights workers–Biography–Juvenile literature.
Classification: LCC PS3551.N464 K4155 2019 | DDC 818'.5409 B–dc23

First Edition

Published in 2019 by
Gareth Stevens Publishing
111 East 14th Street, Suite 349
New York, NY 10003

Copyright © 2019 Gareth Stevens Publishing

Designer: Katelyn E. Reynolds
Editor: Joshua Turner

Photo credits: Cover, pp. 1 (Maya Angelou), 9 Michael Ochs Archives/Getty Images; cover, pp. 1–32 (background image) Neilson Barnard/Getty Images; p. 5 Ken Charnock/Getty Images; p. 7 LittleT889/Wikipedia.org; p. 8 Mathew Imaging/FilmMagic/Getty Images; p. 11 Gene Lester/Getty Images; p. 13 WALTER DHLADHLA/AFP/Getty Images; p. 15 Vernon Shibla/New York Post Archives /(c) NYP Holdings, Inc. via Getty Images; p. 16 Jack Sotomayor/New York Times Co./Getty Images; p. 17 Craig Herndon / The Washington Post via Getty Images; p. 19 Afro American Newspapers/Gado/Getty Images; p. 21 Don Perdue/Liaison/Getty Images; p. 23 Consolidated News Pictures/Hulton Archive/Getty Images; p. 25 Deborah Feingold/Corbis via Getty Images; p. 27 Andrew Harrer/Bloomberg via Getty Images.

Printed in the United States of America

CPSIA compliance information: Batch #CW19GS: For further information contact Gareth Stevens, New York, New York at 1-800-542-2595.

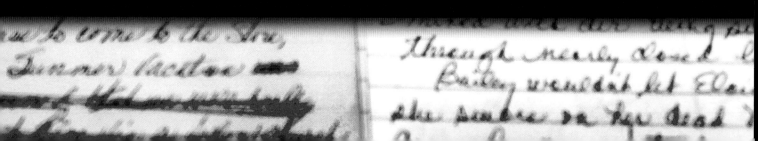

CONTENTS

Words in the glossary appear in **bold** type the first time they are used in the text.

SO MANY RAINBOWS

On April 4, 1928, Marguerite Annie Johnson was born in St. Louis, Missouri. Over the next 86 years, she would grow to become a remarkable woman: an author, a poet, a singer, a composer, a dancer, an actress, a historian, a playwright, a teacher, a director, and an **activist**.

The world would come to know her as Maya Angelou, and her words touched thousands of people during her life. Angelou inspired countless people with her works, both in spite of and because of the challenges in her life. "I've had a lot of clouds," she said, "but I have had so many rainbows."

FROM THE START

Angelou said that she started writing in a journal as a young girl. She wrote essays, or short pieces of writing about her thoughts and opinions, and she wrote poetry. She said later, "of course it was terrible" at that time. But she didn't stop! Today, she's remembered as one of America's most beloved writers.

Maya Angelou is best known as a writer, but she did many things in her life. "We delight in the beauty of the butterfly," she said once, "but rarely admit the changes it has gone through to achieve that beauty."

5

THE CAGED BIRD

Young Marguerite Johnson didn't see her mother much. After her parents split up, her grandmother, Annie Henderson, cared for her and her older brother, Bailey, while they lived in the small country town of Stamps, Arkansas.

The 7-year-old Marguerite was living with her mother in St. Louis when her mother's boyfriend attacked and hurt her. After she told someone about the attack, someone killed the man. Scared that her words had caused the man's death, Marguerite didn't speak again for years. She kept learning, though. She memorized poetry and read many things. In time, she began to talk again.

MRS. FLOWERS

Marguerite returned to Stamps and her grandmother after the attack. After some time, a woman named Bertha Flowers, a friend of her family, began to bring her out of her shell. Mrs. Flowers befriended the girl and gave her some books and poems, telling her to read them out loud.

Marguerite Johnson, later known as Maya Angelou, was born in this building in St. Louis. Her parents were Vivian and Bailey Johnson.

7

MISTRESS OF ALL TRADES

In 1940, when she was 12, the girl who would become Maya Angelou moved to San Francisco, California, with her mother. As she grew older, she held many different jobs. Early on, she worked as a waitress and a cook. She worked taking paint off cars. She was even briefly a cable car conductor in San Francisco—the first African American woman to do so.

She also took classes and was employed as a dancer. And as a dancer in the 1950s, Marguerite Johnson took the name she'd be remembered by. "Maya" was her childhood nickname, and "Angelou" came from "Angelos," the last name of her husband at the time.

IN HER LIGHT

When she was 17 years old, Maya Angelou gave birth to her son, Clyde Johnson, who goes by the name Guy. She raised him by herself, with some help from her mother. Today, Guy Johnson is an author and poet himself. Maya called him "my greatest blessing."

Maya with her son, Guy, in 2005

During an interview in 2003, Maya Angelou said she thought people could learn many different things. "I think you can be a jack-of-all-trades and a mistress-of-all-trades," she said.

9

SINGING, ACTING, WRITING

During the 1950s, Maya moved to New York City and became better known as a performer. She landed a role in the musical *Porgy and Bess* and toured throughout the world in 1954 and 1955. She appeared in other shows, continued to study dance and sing in clubs, and released a music album called *Miss Calypso* in 1957.

FRIENDSHIP WITH KING

After meeting Dr. Martin Luther King Jr., Maya began to work for civil rights with other activists of the time. She became a leader in King's Southern Christian Leadership Conference. After King was **assassinated** on her birthday, April 4, in 1968, Maya didn't celebrate her birthday for many years. She sent flowers to his widow instead.

The woman who once wrote "terrible poetry" as a girl was still writing, too. Maya joined the Harlem Writers Guild at this time. She met author James Baldwin and also heard civil rights activist Dr. Martin Luther King Jr. speak.

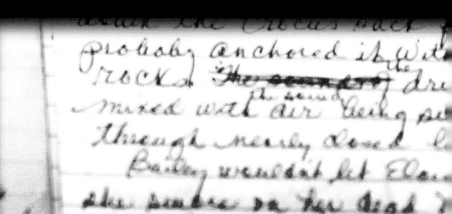

This photo was taken at the photo shoot for the cover of Maya's 1957 album *Miss Calypso*.

IN AFRICA

In 1961, Maya and her son moved to Cairo, Egypt. There, she started writing for a living—not poetry, but reports for a newspaper called the *Arab Observer*. Then she moved to Accra, Ghana, and wrote and edited for the *African Review*.

As a **journalist**, Maya met many important African Americans during her time in Africa, including activist W. E. B. Du Bois and freedom fighter Nelson Mandela in 1962. In an interview in 1992, Maya said she still considered Africa "a part of home" and spoke about how good it was to find familiar things there.

MALCOLM X

Maya met activist Malcolm X when he visited Ghana from the United States. This meeting led, in 1965, to her return to the United States, where she helped him create his civil rights group, the Organization of Afro-American Unity. The group fell apart, however, when Malcolm X was assassinated.

Nelson Mandela, shown, **recited** Maya's poem "Still I Rise"
when he was sworn into office as president of South Africa in 1994.
Maya wrote the poem "His Day Is Done" in 2013 when Mandela died.

THE STORIES OF HER LIFE

After Maya returned to the United States, friends, including author James Baldwin and editor Robert Loomis, encouraged her to write an **autobiography**, telling the story of her life so far. But Angelou wanted to write plays and poems, so she said no.

In time, however, she reconsidered and she began working on a **memoir**. *I Know Why the Caged Bird Sings* was published in 1969. It tells the story of her youth and deals with many themes, including the attack she endured as a girl, her silent years, and growing up black amidst the **racism** of the South.

"SYMPATHY"

The title of Maya Angelou's first memoir comes from "Sympathy," a poem by African American poet Paul Laurence Dunbar. Dunbar was one of the authors whose work young Marguerite Johnson read during the years she didn't speak. She also read works by W. E. B. Du Bois, whom she'd later meet in Ghana, and many others.

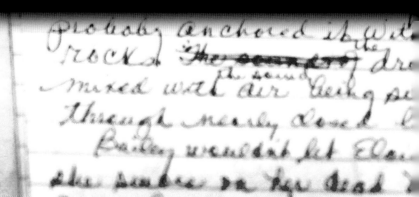

I Know Why the Caged Bird Sings follows Maya's life up until the birth of her son when she was 17 years old.

I Know Why the Caged Bird Sings was a great success and earned Maya much fame. It was **nominated** for a National Book Award and became the first **nonfiction** best seller by an African American woman. In 1979, CBS aired a made-for-TV movie based on the book. Maya helped write the movie.

She went on to write more autobiographies: *Gather Together in My Name* (1974), *Singin' and Swingin' and Gettin' Merry Like Christmas* (1976), *The Heart of a Woman* (1981), *All God's Children Need Traveling Shoes* (1986), and *A Song Flung Up to Heaven* (2002). The first, however, is still her most widely read work.

CAGED BIRD IN SCHOOLS

I Know Why the Caged Bird Sings is an American classic, and is often taught in US schools. However, some of its content, including Maya's words about how she was attacked as a child, make it **controversial** to some people. It's one of the most challenged or banned books in US schools.

16

Maya during an interview in 1978

According to editor Robert Loomis, after Maya Angelou first decided against writing a memoir, he called her back and told her it was "nearly impossible to write autobiography as **literature**." She took it as a challenge.

FINDING THE WORDS

Maya kept writing, and the words did not stop. The woman who was once a girl who wanted to be a poet published her first book of poetry, *Just Give Me a Cool Drink of Water 'fore I Diiie*, in 1971. It was followed by many more, including *And Still I Rise* in 1978.

She'd also wanted to write plays, and she did that too, in a way. In 1968, *Black, Blues, Black!* a 10-part series written by Maya, aired on television. And in 1972, Maya became one of the first African American women to have a screenplay, or the written form of a movie, produced, with the film *Georgia, Georgia*.

A COOL DRINK OF WATER

Maya's first book of poetry contains 38 poems. They touch on a number of themes, including love and the lives of black people throughout the years in the United States. The book was nominated for a Pulitzer Prize for Poetry in 1972.

Of all her accomplishments, Maya said she was most happy to be a writer. Here, she receives an award in 1981.

STAGE AND SCREEN

Even as she wrote, Maya kept performing. In 1977, she was part of the cast in the TV adaptation of the novel *Roots*, which tells the story of seven generations of an African and African American family. She was nominated for an Emmy Award for her role. Emmy Awards honor accomplishments in American television productions.

Maya also appeared in the movie *Poetic Justice* (for which she also wrote poetry) in 1993, the television movie *There Are No Children Here* in 1993, and the movie *How to Make an American Quilt* in 1995. In 1998, at 70 years old, she tried something new, directing the movie *Down in the Delta*.

TONY NOMINEE

In 1973, Maya appeared in *Look Away*, a Broadway play about Mary Todd Lincoln. Although the show closed after only one Broadway performance, she was nominated for a Tony Award, which honors accomplishments in American theater.

Maya also had a part in Tyler Perry's *Medea's Family Reunion*, which came out in 2006. In it, she recites her poem "In and Out of Time."

PRESIDENTIAL POETRY

In January 1993, Maya made history in yet another way. She became the first person since 1961 to recite a poem at the **inauguration** of a US president when she read her work "On the Pulse of Morning" at President Bill Clinton's inauguration ceremony.

This was the first time a poet had presented such a work at an inauguration since Robert Frost read "The Gift Outright" for President John F. Kennedy. "In my work, in everything I do, I mean to say that we human beings are more alike than we are unalike," Maya said at the time.

INAUGURAL INSPIRATION

Even though Maya Angelou was already a famous poet in 1993, she was still nervous about reading a poem for the inauguration. She told an interviewer that to prepare to write it, she read aloud from other works by authors who had inspired her, including Frederick Douglass, Patrick Henry, and Thomas Paine.

Maya was the first African American and the first woman to read a poem at a US presidential inauguration. In 2009, poet Elizabeth Alexander became the second when she read "Praise Song for the Day" at Barack Obama's inauguration.

23

DR. ANGELOU

Maya never went to college, but college did come to her. In 1981, she became a professor of American studies at Wake Forest University in Winston-Salem, North Carolina, where she taught for many years. In a 1993 interview with the *New York Times*, she said the job gave her "a large umbrella," adding that "a lot of people stand under it. A lot of young blacks and whites and students and some plain, some tall, some very, very smart and some slow."

Even though she didn't have a **doctorate**, many people came to call her "Dr. Angelou." She received more than 50 honorary **degrees** in her lifetime.

ALL THE WORDS

Maya Angelou never seemed to run out of words. In addition to her autobiographies and books of poetry, she wrote other books, individual poems, and more essays. Her work included a few children's books, such as *Life Doesn't Frighten Me* in 1998. She also wrote two cookbooks. She even wrote greeting cards for Hallmark!

24

THE MANY WORDS OF MAYA ANGELOU

Maya Angelou was a prolific author. That means she wrote many things. These are only some of the many books and books of poems she wrote.

I Know Why the Caged Bird Sings (1969)

Just Give Me a Cool Drink of Water 'fore I Diiie (1971)

Gather Together in My Name (1974)

Singin' and Swingin' and Gettin' Merry Like Christmas (1976)

And Still I Rise (1978)

The Heart of a Woman (1981)

All God's Children Need Traveling Shoes (1986)

Now Sheba Sings the Song (1987)

I Shall Not Be Moved (1990)

Wouldn't Take Nothing for My Journey Now (1993)

My Painted House, My Friendly Chicken, and Me (1994)

Life Doesn't Frighten Me (1998)

A Song Flung Up to Heaven (2002)

Letter to My Daughter (2008)

Mom & Me & Mom (2013)

HIGH HONORS

Some people slow down in their 70s and 80s. If Maya Angelou did, it wasn't very noticeable! She kept writing, and she kept earning awards. In 2000, President Bill Clinton presented her with the National Medal of Arts. In 2005 and 2009, she won NAACP Image Awards. In 2013, she received the Literarian Award for contributions to the literary community.

In 2011, President Barack Obama presented Maya with the Presidential Medal of Freedom. This is the highest award that can be presented to a civilian, or someone who isn't a member of the military, in the United States.

GRAMMYS

Although Maya was best known for her writing, she also won three Grammy Awards. Grammys are usually presented for accomplishments in the music field, but Maya's awards (in 1993, 1995, and 2002) were for the best spoken-word album for three recited poetry recordings.

In this photo, President Barack Obama gives Maya Angelou a kiss after he presented her with the Presidential Medal of Freedom in 2011.

27

THE POETRY OF COURAGE

Maya Angelou, poet and writer and speaker and so much more, died on May 28, 2014. She was 86 years old. She left behind countless written words and performances that inspired and touched people around the world.

First Lady Michelle Obama, actress and TV host Oprah Winfrey, and former president Bill Clinton were among the thousands of people who attended Maya's memorial service at Wake Forest University. "She taught me the poetry of courage and respect," Winfrey said at the service. "We can be better and do better because she existed."

IN MEMORY

President Barack Obama released a statement in 2014 when Maya died. He said, in part: "Over the course of her remarkable life, Maya was many things—an author, poet, civil rights activist, playwright, actress, director, composer, singer, and dancer. But above all, she was a storyteller—and her greatest stories were true."

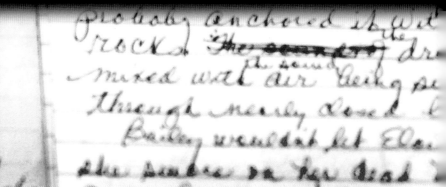

THE LIFE OF MAYA ANGELOU

1928 Marguerite Annie Johnson is born on April 4th in St. Louis, Missouri.

1940 Johnson moves to San Francisco, California, with her mother.

1945 Johnson's son, Clyde "Guy" Johnson, is born.

1954 Johnson, now called Maya Angelou, begins touring as part of the musical *Porgy and Bess*.

1957 Angelou releases an album, *Miss Calypso*.

1961 Angelou moves to Cairo.

1965 Angelou returns to the United States.

1969 *I Know Why the Caged Bird Sings*, Angelou's first autobiography, is published.

1971 Angelou appears on Broadway in *Look Away* and is nominated for a Tony Award.

1977 Angelou appears in *Roots*.

1979 A movie based on *I Know Why the Caged Bird Sings* airs on television.

1981 Angelou becomes a professor of American studies at Wake Forest University.

1993 Angelou recites her poem "On the Pulse of Morning" at Bill Clinton's inauguration.

1998 Angelou directs *Down in the Delta*.

2000 Angelou receives the National Medal of Arts.

2002 Angelou's final autobiography is published.

2011 Angelou receives the Presidential Medal of Freedom.

2014 Maya Angelou dies on May 28th at age 86.

GLOSSARY

activist: one who acts strongly in support of or against an issue

assassinate: to kill someone, especially a public figure

autobiography: a book written by someone about his or her own life

controversial: causing arguments

degree: an official title given to someone who has completed a course of study at a college or university

doctorate: the highest degree offered by a university, which requires many years of study

inauguration: when a president is sworn in and takes the oath of office

journalist: someone who works with the collecting, writing, and editing of news stories for newspapers, magazines, websites, television, or radio

literature: written works considered to be very good and important

memoir: a written account in which someone describes his or her past experiences

nominate: to suggest someone for an honor

nonfiction: writing that is based on facts or real things that have happened

racism: the belief that people of different races have different qualities and abilities and that some are superior or inferior

recite: to read or say something out loud

FOR MORE INFORMATION

BOOKS

Angelou, Maya. *Life Doesn't Frighten Me.* 25th anniversary ed. New York, NY: Abrams Books for Young Readers, 2017.

Labrecque, Ellen. *Who Was Maya Angelou?* New York, NY: Grosset & Dunlap, 2016.

Wilson, Edwin Graves. *Poetry for Young People: Maya Angelou.* New York, NY: Sterling Children's Books, 2013.

WEBSITES

Biography: Maya Angelou
www.ducksters.com/biography/authors/mayaangelou.php
Ducksters provides a biography of Maya Angelou on this popular site.

BrainPOP: Maya Angelou
www.brainpop.com/english/famousauthorsandbooks/mayaangelou/
This website offers a short animated movie and more information on Maya Angelou's life.

Caged Bird Legacy
www.mayaangelou.com/
The official Maya Angelou website offers a message from her family and more information on her life and books.

INDEX